planes, birds, cats, things

David Kelly

planes, birds, cats, things

Acknowledgements

Some of these poems have appeared in the following journals:
Southerly, Bardfly, Redoubt, Ulitarra, Sidewalk, Saltlick, Going Down Swinging, Island, Famous Reporter, Five by Five, tamba, Shepparton News, Woorilla and *Black Inc's Best Australian Poems 2004.*

'The big stumps at Cambarville' was Highly Commended
in the 2005 Woorilla Poetry Prize.

planes, birds, cats, things
ISBN 978 1 76109 193 3
Copyright © text David Kelly 2021
Cover image: *Saturn* by Dennis Spiteri (www.dennis-spiteri.com)

First published 2021 by
GINNINDERRA PRESS
PO Box 3461 Port Adelaide 5015
www.ginninderrapress.com.au

Contents

Introduction	9
planes	
Like blood	13
Something about it	14
Bring on the clouds	15
What	16
Nightbirds	18
Tricks	19
Concorde	20
It's all in the numbers	21
The people up the front	22
Nostalgia	23
On the wing	24
Nightmare	26
Down safe	28
Flying home on Virgin Blue	30
What aeroplanes do to air	32
Pods	33
Rapture	34
birds	
Better than Saturn	37
Gang-gangs	38
Ibises	39
Rare bird	40
The big stumps at Cambarville	42
Duck work	44
King parrot	45
Sulphur-crested cockatoos	46
Visitors	47

Magpies	49
Grubs and bugs	53
Chicken shed	54
Met the chicken	56
Yellow-tailed black cockatoos	58
Bird-happy	62

cats

Bobby	65
Little Cat	68
Two halves of the one cat	70
Little was a good jumper	72
The pissing incident	74
Grey's operation	76
Little Cat dies	78
Black and White's birthday bash	79
Triangle	82
Two for White and Black	84

things

Coca Cola	89
Stapler	90
Sellotape dispenser	91
Calculator	92
CD player	94
Filing cabinet	95
Digital clocks	96
Children's clock	97
The old moon	98
Rainbows	99
Black purse	100
Handbag	101
Hairbrush	102

Biker jacket	103
Supermarket trolley	104
Radio	105
Frame	106
Lectern	107
Lawnmower	108
Axe	110
Taps	111
Automatic vacuum cleaner	113
Mouse	114
Electric radiator	115
Thongs graveyard	116
Fireworks	118
Chrysler Regal Station Wagon	120

Introduction

the punctuation anomaly

These poems stretch back over almost thirty years, with the 'things' section dating from the early 1990s. Readers will notice the 'planes' and 'birds' sections have no punctuation, 'cats' has (mostly) conventional punctuation and 'things' has a manic reliance on the semicolon. There is no real explanation for the difference. It was just the way I was feeling when I wrote them so I've kept them as they were.

thanks to

Helene Castles, Tug Dumbly and Kris Hemensley for advice and back cover praise.

Dennis Spiteri for allowing me to use Saturn from his *The Planets* series to supercharge the cover.

Members of the Goulburn Valley Writers' Group and Myron Lysenko's Woodend Chamber Poets.

Special thanks to Grey Cat, Little Cat, Bobby, Triangle, Black Tom, Black-and-White and White-and-Black and a few more cats that didn't make their way into poems!

extra special gold label thanks to

Pippa Driscoll and Heimana 'Dave' Raufauore.

planes

Like blood

as it flies
flexing in air
out to the wingtips
moving the flaps
and back
out to all the lights
blinking and back
in the pilot's egg
of the blunt nose
guidance radio radar
through the length of it
as it flies
all around
the warm drowsy
hatchery of passengers
through kilometres of wires
circuits and circles
lungs kidneys bladder
as it flies
flexing in air
electricity
flows through it
like blood

Something about it

something about the way it glides
over the beer garden of the corner pub
and the long sleek white belly
is plumb to heaven
and you could almost reach up
with a long handled broom
and stroke it as it passed
something about the way
it floats down its final approach
wingtips trembling and tilting
like a real bird
something in the muscular
thickness of wings and body
the windows at the front
the yelp of its landing
makes me want to sneak on board
when everyone has left
walk up the narrow aisle
of the dim cabin
and squeeze the seats

Bring on the clouds

we're all sitting there
bolt upright
we've done the seat belt
stowed everything away
watched the safety show
yellow oxygen cones
Marcel Marceau
then the buffeting run
we're all in it
like a Flintstones bus
legs through the floor
grinning to each other
this is what we paid for
arms pumping at the big
strapped on wings
run pump   run pump   run pump
it's lifting
it's lifting
that big backward tilt
and bring on the clouds

grand final mad
we turn to each other
fists in the air   winking
long sighs   palm slaps
we pull our legs up
tuck them under the seats
grown men crying
we shake our arms loose
and let the crew take over

What

when we go somewhere
in an aeroplane
first we have to walk down
a long rectangular corridor
black rubber mat
blue textured cloth on the walls
photos of sporting heroes
we come to a doorway
where people in uniforms
stand and smile at us
we go into something
like a big long cinema
with little windows
so we can see the screen
which is all around us
they show a documentary
Clouds and Landscape
and make lots of roaring
and thumping sounds
they serve us food tea coffee etc
after an hour or so
we all get up and leave
people in uniforms
stand at the door and smile at us

we walk down a long
rectangular corridor
photos of sporting heroes
blue textured cloth on the walls
black rubber mat

what are we being prepared for

Nightbirds

I often go out
and watch them
fly over my house
to the airport
as if they're coming home
tight wires
of electric instinct
winch them in
their big lights blare
and the suburb
hums beneath them
like a tuning fork
maybe one or two
will stop for an hour
before New Zealand
but most of them
bed down and huddle
in a white flock
against the dark and cold
they switch off and go quiet
their feet get chocked
they sink into their springs
a slow night mist
forms a wet sheen
all over their tails
their long bodies
their wings
their engine pods

Tricks

have you ever seen them
stalking an airport
on a damp grey afternoon
fluffy white scarves
trailing off their wings
that's one of their
better tricks
the full repertoire
is stunning of course
loop the loop
break the sound barrier
and just staying up's
a pretty good act
when you consider
the wings don't flap
and you can't see
too many moving parts
all the air's their catwalk
and they surge through it
as arrogant as supermodels
their inner fire
their cold outer shell

Concorde

announcing the gift of itself
with the howl of a thousand crows
and no thought of pardon please may I
to my front yard sky or the banana trees
struggling by the side fence
a Concorde flew over the other day
an intergalactic movie just for me
at the time it seemed
hard to believe anything
so huge could move that slowly
and yet stay up
and I imagined all sorts
of impossibly cumbersome things
lumbering through the air of
Annandale NSW
the rattling centipede
of a Northern Territory cattle train
an oil tanker dripping tears of ocean
onto roads and roof tiles
or a winged Clydesdale
pulling a trotting harness
with a whip-chick Qantas blonde in it
but oh those wings triangular
that set to peck angle
that penetrant beak

It's all in the numbers

of simple and complex
arithmetic on bits of paper
pencil doodlings
computer printouts
3-4-5 triangles
pi   catenary curves
fractions and percentages
and then fingers and metal
are important of course
and plastic and rubber
and carpets and paint
and welders and saws
and rivet guns
and knees and shoulders
and greasy blue overalls
and a third hand
never go astray
when making anything
but get it right
cut true to the plan
with the rivets
5cm apart not 6cm
and the curves just so
not close but spot on
to the printed doodle

that's what the plane is
it's all that number and geometry
on bits of paper

The people up the front

there are some people
sitting right up the front
in blue and gold coats
as we speak they're
looking out the window
checking the stars
checking the gauges
it'll all work out
they're constantly training
and they put every new crash
in the simulators to make sure
it'll never happen again

calm down mate
stop pacing the aisle
you're scaring the passengers
sit in your seat
watch the movie
eat your stalks
pick your fleas

don't panic gorilla
the people up the front
know exactly where we're going
and how to get us there

Nostalgia

I read somewhere
that when the clocks
tick over to 2000
you shouldn't be flying
in an aeroplane
it could be a case of
four…three…two…one…
downski
I've also read
there isn't enough
parking space at the airports
for all the aeroplanes
so some of them
will have to be
in the air that night
the earlier models of course
rattling rivets   flaking paint
seating and fixtures removed
in the Lang Syne darkness
with the navy watching
they'll circle off shore
the oldest planes
the oldest pilots
four…three…two…

On the wing

a clear sign black paint
neat Helvetica-style letters
Do not stand in this area
and at this height no one is
but the lack of handholds
on the silver plumage
bothers me a lot
for if by foul chance
you should find yourself
alone out there
your only hope would be
to push your arms
over the thick curve
of the leading edge
and hang on for grim
this particular plane
has a little raised bump
at the far edge of the wing
but it's just the promise of a hand hold
and the short aerial poking
out of it would snap
if you grabbed it

anyway
handrails footrests and safety straps
combined wouldn't help you
we're as high as Everest
you'd freeze out there
be clinka-clinka
by the time we landed
better to have slippery-dipped
down the wing at take off
and burst your bum on the tarmac
damaged goods
but still alive

Nightmare

the plane landed
and I was in it
the thrust
roared and roared
and the big room
slowed to the bus speed
where we all think
we're safe now
but then a tyre blew
and the plane spun around
tilted tail first
into a canal
beside the runway
and started to sink at 45
us going down
with our backs to hell
it sank as calm
as a ghost might
the damned canal
deep at this point
and I thought – *Ah no
we're all goners* –
as it kept slipping
centimetre by centimetre
into the old canal
the green-scummed canal

so shoulder-shoved me
against all the rest
in the wet dark
rat-ran me
the black aisle up
to save me
to save me

Down safe

she'll feel the downing
begin a half hour out
she'll feel the engines
working less   feel the plane
make friends with gravity
she'll see a familiar
bit of coast   a bend of river
then the seat belt lights
will make their little pings
and Captain Rumblevoice
will promise to have her
on the ground in Adelaide
at seven twenty-three
she'll sink into her seat
watch roads and buildings
known from childhood
then the new freeway
lots of grass
the black of the runway
the thuddy thud thud
the wind breaks howling
no skating or sliding
but a perfect straight run
and suddenly she's in a huge
warm bus rolling
eggshell safe
to the terminal

a few minutes later
with her matted hair
daggy green jumper
and that frazzled backpack
she'll walk smiling
from the long quiet
birth canal of Gate 15
and fall into
that old automatic
welcoming hug
she does with him

Flying home on Virgin Blue

you walk to the plane
across the asphalt
open air like *Casablanca*
the engines are idling
the fans spinning
slowly in their cowls
as you climb up
the stair ramp and step inside
if it should be raining
so much the better
more like the old days

you'll turn back and wave
once
quick
to the woman
wispy hair   damp coat
hand squeeze
Safe travel she'd said

so when you sit
cramped and numb
and still steamy
from the rain
and the bright young attendants
have packed and closed
and it's rolling down
to clearance
and the captain's telling it
you know that everything
really will be all right

it's a big dipper
with wings
happy screaming faces
waving arms
going up and over
and rushing down
a huge rainbow
BNE to SYD

they'll get you home

they do this every day

What aeroplanes do to air

they bully their way
around the air
they suck it in and blow it out
like body builders
with big Mr Universe muscles
on their wings
they use the air like bastards
and the silly air keeps them up
groaning and crying and whinging
some excuse about a vacuum
on the upper curve of the wing
but it's only got itself to blame
and secretly it throbs that
24 – 365
they're sliding in

Pods

they don't
hang off the plane
so much as the plane
sits on them
but can you imagine
those hot little pods
with a life of their own
wouldn't it be
hotter still if
after the hard yards
of take off
during the bullet climb
they slunk up and back
maybe a bit to the side
and tucked themselves
under the wing
to make the plane
look like a real bird
all thrusty
and puffing its chest

Rapture

can't be much
longer now before
the planes will ditch
that embarrassing
old-fashioned
charging bull thing
they do down the tarmac
to get airborne
and they'll learn to rise
in a more evolved
almost seraphic manner

after everyone's on board
they'll pull back
from the loading tube
and levitate
balloon Buddha
Grand Master
then they'll fold up
their landing legs
glide through the heat haze
in an out of body kind of way
queue quietly
breathe in slowly
breathe out slowly
suck velocity
from the very air
swindle gravity
become metal wind

birds

Better than Saturn

at the Cascades near Leura
my girlfriend and I
were looking over the valley
at sunset and all the birds
started singing and calling
and whistling to each other
they switched on like a radio

they do it at sunrise too
of course and we thought
there must be a ring of it
up through China and Russia
and down the other side
all around the world
even over the oceans
the wide winged birds
and the flightless birds
on the sprinkled islands

Earth spins through
a bracelet of bird song

it's better than Saturn

Gang-gangs

two gang-gangs
are creaking their hinges
and gutsing red berries
on a front yard tree
they let me stand very close
and ignore me
don't even bother to look at me
I'm interested because
I haven't seen gang-gangs
here before and as Madonna said –
rejection's a great aphrodisiac

I ask the male
Why the hot-pink helmet?
either he hasn't heard me
or doesn't want to…

…but SHE stops mid squeeze
of a bright red berry
turns into the sun
which ignites the salmon subplot
of her pale grey pine-cone body
dips her head down my way and asks
Where's your tail?
All the other wallabies have one

Ibises

two ibises land in the backyard
white horizontal teardrops
on red legs like short stilts
on top of all that
there's a grey head
with an unnecessarily elongated beak
in the curve of a quill
also grey and…
…or if perhaps a carver had shaped it
he would run his hand along the curve
eye it in all directions
declare it finished
and perfect enough to play music through

my little black and white cat
is optimistically stalking them
one of them gives her a Tyson look

what do they find to eat in mud?

their heads are jigging back and forth
as if sniffing out what lies ahead
snatching a breath of what's to come
and then pulling back
for a lungful of the certainties of now

they are rock and rolling in and out of soon
mesmerising themselves and me and the cat
who on assessment is content to watch
these feathered metronomes
conducting the future
through their long improbable beaks

Rare bird

a small bird
like a pardalote
a robin or a chat
flies past and lands
in the lemon tree
how curious it is
its little head
swivels constantly
its chest is
greenish black
like an avocado
with a similar
curve and taper
though smaller

my heart pumps up
Moon-big
I offer total love
swear I will
do anything for it
but though I beg quietly
Please stay longer
it hits the wing

later when I check
in the heaviest
of my bird books
I find the adored

shy and reclusive
very little known
occasional visitor
to rural backyards
one spherical brown egg
sometimes called
Avocado Bird

The big stumps at Cambarville

the sign calls it
an historic village
but it's just a clear space
of long grass
with about a dozen
big rot-grey stumps
that look like
termite mounds
it's the size of a small town's
cricket field
perhaps the village green
but more likely a tent city
for the timber cutters
and you can still see
the notches where those men
jammed their planks in
swung their axes
and killed the king trees
kings hang out with kings
like attracts like sadly
maybe if they'd spread
themselves around more
but then…maybe not

the notches seem like
stylised eyes and mouths
on god statues
one of the big stumps
is nearly two metres across
most are around two metres high
the ankle bones of tall trees
they could be ruins from the Incas
or the Fertile Crescent
but this is Australian archaeology
and the big stumps
are all that's left
of an old green city
its wind creak and bird whistle
its high leafy suburbs
possum cough and snake trade
the cockatoo wars of 1623

Duck work

a serious looking mother duck
of a drab brown sparrow colour
with ten creamy white ducklings
each about the size of two thumbs
is skimming past the end of a jetty
the seven people there rise and look
Oh yes… Down there… Lovely…
then resettle to wait for the ferry
the ducklings buoyant and obedient
push their little thumbnail feet
exhaustingly through the water
they're packed tight to the mother
on the side of her away from the jetty
and away from the clucky people

strict mother duck leads her brood
to a new nest or a mud flat lunch
and swims just fast enough that they
creamy and fluffy and breathing hard
learn water sense and duck striving
she's wise and calm and as they grow
and darken she'll tell them
of preening and feeding and safety
and all the subtleties of duck work

King parrot

you couldn't blame a king parrot
picking through its velvety
red green and blue-purple feathers
if it thought the bush was drab
the fungi that glow scarlet
and yellow are mostly small
and out of the way
the best flowers have short seasons
the honeycomb brightness
of freshly cracked sandstone
soon fades into the background
of blurred dirty pastels
of dusty greens greys and browns

there's one now

it flaps off a skinny branch
and colour bombs the bush
the outspread wings reveal
a light green zigzag bar
distinctly king parrot
a thick line of unique blue-purple
divides the main red and green
and that red is not the red
of fire engines embers or carnations
nor is that green the green
of apples bottles or Ireland
it strafes the McCubbin coloured bush
with an iridescent blur
of king parrot red
and king parrot green
and you couldn't blame it

Sulphur-crested cockatoos

in the tree near my deck
three white cockatoos
wait Hitchcock-quiet
for me to feed them

then one unfurls
its sulphur crest
as an Opera House
of bananas

after the sun had
stroked their heads
it left itself behind
in freehand plumes

what did
the cockatoo
say to Leunig
Drorr…drorr…

is the one who is
the largest today
the same one who was
the largest yesterday

they wait…

therefore they think

Visitors

to me fifteen
red-green firecrackers
exploding across
the long flat veranda rail

to the fifteen happy
king parrots a pit stop
on a pub crawl
handfuls of grey
sunflower seed
taken on tab

one bird jumps
to each hand
and to keep stable
they sink their claws
so delicately and precisely
as not to pierce the skin
I tense into stillness
and my hands grow heavy

do they think I'm something
like a free-moving tree
or do they say to each other
that I too am warm
and pulse like they do?

all at once and altogether
an urgent flapping of wings
and lots of squawking
and they're gone
where?
grass heads on a roadside
an orchard
the picnic ground

I don't think they'll
tremble like I did in afterglow
to them I was just
another Mine Host
a lower order seed-god

Magpies

they are born pink, naked and blind
with large feet, a short broad beak
and a bright red throat

gymnorhina tibicen tibicen
(bare-nosed flute-player flute-player)
the 'nominate' form
so musical it had to be named twice
gymnorhina tibicen tyrannica
(bare-nosed flute-player bully)
a large white-backed kind found in Victoria
(though according to locals
not lately in Euroa)
seven others at last count

while it is slowly stalking
across the nearby table
rough grey wood
at the outdoor restaurant
it is also classifying you

wardle woodle koo koo
(sitting bulky curious)
many humans unable to forage for themselves
gather in small numbers to be fed
by the more active members of the tribe

short femur (above knee)
and relatively long lower leg
restrict its ability to hop
(c/f e.g. the blue/brown wren)
hence the constant walking
with brief bursts of running

up north they have learned
to flip cane-toads onto their backs
and rip out their bellies
the cane toads weep at this point
(who cares) *Go Magpies*

before they learn about
getting-out-of-the-way
many littlies/new-borns
become country-roadkill
Greg Hughes of Euroa
calls October–November
the season of young dead Magpies

mighty Collingwood AFL
mighty Euroa (Vic) AFL
mighty Hawkes Bay (NZ) Union
mighty Newcastle United (UK) Soccer
mighty Souths Logan (Qld) League
mighty Western Suburbs (NSW) League (gone now)
mighty Glenorchy (Tas) AFL (controversial)
Go 'Pies… Go 'Pies… Go 'Pies…

the selfish beak
prods the cornucopic dirt
for beetles   grubs   worms
grasshoppers   spiders
any bug in a garden
magpie beaks are easy-pleasey-beaks
small frogs   lizards   snakes
cockroaches and centipedes
larvae waiting preconsciously
and any handout from
the sitting bulky curious

given they'll eat just about anything
and we love 'em to bits
they've a fairly good chance
of long term survival

complex melodious warbles
pitched at 2–4 kHz
do not carry long distances
up to 70 minutes
calls recorded for the approach
of eagles and monitor lizards

we've all seen a young one
strutting back and forth
cuddling its aural teddy bear
we've all been grateful
for the Christmas present
of endless magpie dawns
and wondered at the enigma
of a black and white bird
with a rainbow song
that blasts the murk of human
self-pity from the air
and how their sound-bites
are far too long bright
and relevant for tv news grabs

they are indeed fleet of flute

they ripple Monet through the air

* Quoted information is taken from the Wikipedia article
'Australian magpie'.

Grubs and bugs

most of the world's small islands
are in the South Pacific
and on those islands
where there are few predators
many of the land based birds
have shrunk their wings
and don't bother to fly any more
it's too strenuous and anyway
far easier to pick grubs and bugs
out of the ground and leaf-rot
than catch mosquitoes flies
and grasshoppers mid-air

a lot of them have developed
the response of standing stock still
trying not to breathe or blink
if they feel threatened
so they probably have something
like a race memory
of being hunted once

when they think
the threat has passed
they'll move once more
resume their life
look for food
build a nest
seek a mate

after a while
it all starts again
it all keeps going on

Chicken shed

the five fat chooks run out
three brown ones two white ones
and Bonzer the little golden bantam
they all start raking up the dirt
one looks at me while it is scratching
like a child showing off
I clean out the shed
scrape the concrete floor
and hose away the old hay
with their droppings stuck through it
then spread out the new hay
and pack it into their nest boxes

meanwhile they've scratched holes
in the soft damp dirt nearby
they sit down and rub dirt into their feathers
then stay still with their feathers
and wings at odd angles
like their wings might be broken
or they look like they might be sick
or even dying but they get up
and wander off together
Bonzer always following behind
they mutter to themselves
in repetitious chook talk
something about the sky and
a big catastrophe
I don't believe them

I do a few odd jobs elsewhere
paint a door   weed a garden
they wander all over the place
my midweek casual day flies past
and soon enough it's time to collect
bread and cabbage and lettuce
and call them back into Cackleberry House
I start calling   *Here chooky…here chooky…*
and find myself talking to them
as they follow me into the shed
though by now they must know
I'll lock the door and leave them in
perhaps they don't mind
realising they're safer that way
little Bonzer is always the last
she runs in with a few cackly screaks
and a fluff and flourish of her clipped wings

Met the chicken

crossing the main road
for my fish and chips the other day
I met a chicken on the refuge island
the traffic was treacherous
we stood there together
looking left and right and left again
she was a good-looking bird
soap-powder white
you wouldn't say plump
but her feathers had
a soft glow like suede
we started talking
she was magnanimous
about the outlooks from the houses
on the eastern side of the street
but disappointed in their backyards
all wheelie bins red brick pavers
Hills Hoists everywhere
and really hard scratching
went on to say she'd heard
encouraging comments about
over-the-road   I didn't want to raise
any false hopes in her
but mentioned that a few places
on the western strip
where I lived had soft lawns
lily ponds   vegie gardens   some even had
compost heaps   in addition
the back yards soaked up the heat
all afternoon and made the living…well…easy

Cool she clucked *can't wait*
the traffic thinned
we promised to keep in touch
before skipping off dodgem quick
to our respective other sides
I paused outside the fish shop
and turned around to see
that she'd made it safely over
and was already pecking
at one of the better-looking doors

Yellow-tailed black cockatoos

we heard the noise first
a drummy rapid thumping
like a helicopter
then looked up in time
to see the invasion
six black cockatoos
with yellow barred tails
and yellow around their eyes
swooped down from nowhere
and took over the trees in front of us
high in a fork one by itself
further along the same branch
more exposed and easier to see
another by itself
close by in a second tree
at the end of a dead branch
two together kissing and
frolicking like lovers
in a third tree a youngster
squawked and squawked
hounding a larger one

we'd left the track and picked
our way to the shoulder
of a thickly wooded Blackheath valley
the ground was steep and rough
mossy sandstone and hollows
of leaf mould broken twigs and so on
we didn't dare move in case
we frightened them and our legs
began to ache as we strained
to keep still on the awkward ground
we held hands supporting each other
craning our upper bodies
to get a better look at them

we wished we could suddenly
become gentle aliens   lift   float
extend ourselves silently
onto the branches where
the big black cockatoos were
they would amble towards us
left claw   right claw   left claw
tilt their yellow patched heads
side to side and greet us with a quiet
crarck…crarck-crarck…
our minds would flow into one
and share the story of
our different ways of being

but no we can't talk to birds yet
they sit loud and peaceful
in the leafy branches and we stand
quiet and awkward on the ground

we watched and listened
as they talked to each other
the lovers circled beak to beak
and chattered in cockatoo
the kid squawked on and on
all the time they
seemed to call and answer
and interrupt each other
until one of them made
a directive…an order…
and the others went quiet
then it sprung off its branch
and thumped away
through the blue air
along the side of the valley

less than a minute later the lovers
took off in the same direction
and soon afterwards
the remaining three flew out
we saw the whole group
briefly on the other side of the valley
and could hear the youngster
carrying on for a long time

we found a large flat rock
close by and stood there
hugging each other before
heading up to the track again
as we picked our way
through the rotting leaves
and mossy rocks we kept a lookout
for snakes and talked about
everything and nothing
in the soft massaging voice
of wingless human lovers

Bird-happy

down the back of the yard
a small bird   grey wings   black stripes
a patch of yellow on its back
and a long honeyeater's beak
was having a ricochet panic
inside the netting
tied around a plum tree

I wondered how to set it free
without slashing the net
there was a bit of an opening
towards the base of the tree
where the net wasn't too tight
and I started to think about how
to shoo it down there
when another one came by
and hovered around like visiting time
each was calling to the other

I can't know if it saw the hole
or was told by the second bird
or just random luck
but before I could do anything
the trapped bird worked its way out
and the two of them scrammed off
as if they were late for something

sonic booms of bird-happy
tore the air to shreds

cats

Bobby

I have to tell you
about Bobby and my guilt.
I found Bobby as a kitten
probably six or seven weeks.
He was under a car in a car park
with a dog sniffing around.
So I shooed the dog away
and picked up the little kitten.
He was mostly black,
small bit of white on the chest.
To cut a long story short
he spent a lot of time
with one of my friends
but she couldn't keep him
and so I moved
from the concrete box unit
I was renting into a flat
above a furniture shop.
I had the use of a big grassy backyard
and at the end of the day
the shop people went home
and I had the building to myself.
It was private, suited my nature
and I could have Bobby there.
We had him done, as they say,
and as he grew up
he never really seemed happy.
If I stroked him too much
he'd grow cranky and bite me.

I think it aroused him
and maybe somehow he sensed
that he was missing something:
hard to say, really.
After a while I thought I'd get him
a friend, and that's when
I brought home another cat.
That was Little Cat but Little Cat
started to dominate Bobby.
He'd always lie right in the centre
at the front of the radiator
pushing Bobby to the side
or finish his food first
and then take Bobby's.
He'd get in the door first.
In many ways it was obvious
he was the dominant cat.
I had Little done too so
it wasn't like he was wilder or bigger.
In fact he was smaller than Bobby.
One night I came home and
Bobby wasn't there.
He never turned up again.
I asked around a bit
and checked the highway
but never saw or heard anything.

I've always thought that
Bobby left…just walked away
and found somewhere else to live
because of the way
Little Cat dominated him
and that maybe, though trying
to help, I caused Bobby
a lot of hurt by bringing Little in.
I'll never know.

Little Cat

Little Cat had a tail
that curved back along his spine
reaching toward his shoulders.
It looked like the handle
of a kettle but you couldn't
pick him up with it.
He was a tawny and brown
tiger striped cat,
the colouring closest to the wild cat.
He was about mid-size,
neither large nor small,
but little when I got him.
After I'd had him done
I often wondered
if he knew my part in it
but he was always
a happy cat so I guess
that, maybe, in his case
if he didn't know
what he was missing
then he didn't miss it.
Still I'd also wonder
from time to time
that if he'd had the choice
of the quiet life with me,
the fresh meat and fish,
the long slow cuddles
and the safe warm bed
or the wilder one –
would he have gone for it?

Gone for scrounge and beg
and slashed ears,
sleeping rough,
the scent of a she cat
on a cold night –
a quick thick jab.

Two halves of the one cat

Little Cat had a friend
called Grey Cat.
They'd curl up together,
a grey comma snuggled
into a tawny question mark.
I have to tell you something
about Grey's first night with us.
I'd rescued Grey from the pound –
same place I'd picked up Little Cat.
Little had been the cutest
most beautiful kitten there,
three quarters grown.
So I picked Grey,
not because she was cute,
but because she was the saddest,
scruffiest, cat-with-no-hope
looking cat in the whole joint.
The night I brought her home
and introduced them
she jumped on Little,
held him down and lick-cleaned his ears.
He didn't resist in any way.
Maybe he was her kitten
or they'd been friends in the pound.
I have an old square snap of them
lying in the sun together.

They're looking
straight at the camera
and he has his head
lifted up looking over her
like a lion protecting
his one cat pride.
One of my friends
thought they were
very different animals
but I always saw them
as two halves of the one cat.

Little was a good jumper

The bedroom overlooked
the highway.
A huge awning covered
the street below
and a fence at the side.
Little was the only cat
who could jump from the fence
up onto the awning.
I had other cats while I lived there.
As well as Little and Grey
there was Bobby and Claudette
and Claudette had kittens
but I'm getting ahead of myself.
Bobby, who was my first cat,
could jump off the awning
down to the fence
as would Grey and Claudette
but, as I said,
only Little would jump up.
One night, being bored, I happened
to climb out the window
onto the awning and walk along it.
Little must have heard me
and he miaowed for me
so I went to the edge in time
to see him make the jump
from the fence to the awning.

It was well over a metre
and from down there
a cat couldn't see
where he was going to land.
I think that's why the others
were scared to do it.
His body stretched out
like it was slow motion
in a documentary
coming up and up and slowly up
and right over the edge
until his front feet
landed leopard quiet and soft
on the corrugated iron.
Then the rest of his body
fell in behind like rubber
finding its shape again.
He gave me his intimate rumbly miaow
and brushed against me.
We walked over the awning together
and climbed into the bedroom
where Grey was waiting.

The pissing incident

Little Cat was always there
when I drove in at night.
I'd hear him jumping up
on the fence from next door,
a light thwack sound
when he landed at the top.
Then he'd miaow
and leap off the fence
and run over to me.
He lived with me for fifteen years
and there are a few stories
but the pissing incident
happened about two or three a.m.
one winter's night.
At the time we were renting
a flat above a shop
with an outside toilet.
I woke with a full bladder
and went downstairs.
It was too cold to go out
so I flopped the old fella
over the washbasin
and it trickled out.
Only Little and me
living there at the time
so it didn't matter.

When I'd finished
I turned the tap on
to wash it clear
and turned the tap off
but still could hear
a water trickling sound.
I checked me but I'd stopped
and the tap was off
so I looked in the bath
and there was Little Cat
squatting over the plughole,
his pale yellow squirt going
straight through
gurgling on the sides.
I don't think he did it too often.
The window was always open
for him to get out.
I think it was just that,
on this particular night,
he felt like joining me.

Grey's operation

Then there was the time
that Grey had her big operation.
I forget the details
but something in her stomach
had to be taken out
and she came back from the vet
with a puffed and swollen belly,
the stitches red and weeping
and she wouldn't even come
in the flat with us the first night
but stayed in the laundry by herself.
I brought her in the second night
and made her sleep in the bedroom.
I had to hold her hand
while she fell asleep.
Fair dinkum, whenever I let go
she'd miaow softly
and reach out for me again.
In the morning she came
down to the kitchen but wouldn't eat.
Little Cat wouldn't eat either.
He looked up at me,
looked at Grey,
let out a howl and ran into the yard.
He'd gone out in sympathy
like a good union cat.

Poor old Grey!
I called her Grey
because she was a grey and white
tiger striped cat
and there was in her nature
something lovable,
something vague,
something…well…grey.
I still think of her as
just about the warmest person
I ever knew and one of the
biggest gifts of my life.

Little Cat dies

When he was around fifteen
Little's internals gave out
and the vet told me,
He's had his nine, mate.
For the previous two or three years
I'd counted each day with him
as a blessing.
After all, many things
can take out a cat:
cars, dogs, diseases,
falling off a roof and so on.
He'd been with me
about a third of my life.
Anyhow…
I brought him back from the vet
and dug a hole in the yard
near some ferns where he liked
to sleep away his days.
I wrapped him in an old T-shirt,
laid him in the grave
with a photo of him and Grey together,
put in some fish for his journey,
scraped the soil back over him
slowly…slowly…
while stroking his cold tawny fur,
stroking his never-warm-again fur
…God knows how many
one-more-times.

Black and White's birthday bash

It was Black and White's birthday
and I'd planned a little treat for her.
I'd kept it a surprise and only
told her on the night
that I'd be taking her up the main road
to a restaurant for dinner.
She was really excited and a little nervous
because she'd never been up the main road before.
We set off about 7.30
and walked up together.
Towards the end I picked her up
and carried her.
When we reached the restaurant
the owner brought out a high stool
for her so she could sit at table level.
He put a small white napkin around her neck.
She looked as cute as could be,
twisting her head in all directions,
looking over everything.
She was surprised there weren't more cats
but I explained it was a people thing
and she accepted that graciously.
She asked me to order for her
and I suggested the chicken soup
followed by barramundi fillets
in a creamy white wine sauce.
She was impressed with the soup alright
and I had to quieten her down
when she started miaowing
about how good it was.

Then came the barra.
Black and White was in heaven;
all she could do to stop
actually jumping
onto the table but I explained
human restaurant etiquette,
that we were out now
and manners were expected.
She calmed down
and ate to her heart's content.
Next we hit the apple pie and cream.
Well, I hit the pie and she hit the cream.
The birthday toast was difficult.
Black and White isn't one for champagne
so I had a glass of house white
and she finished with a saucer
of house milk and vodka.
She became very cuddly and giggly
and a bit unsteady on her feet.
I took her home in a taxi.
As a further surprise
I'd taken out a documentary
on lions from the video shop.
She'd been asking about this for some time.
We sat on the lounge and watched it together.
She loved it – we ran it through twice.
Finally it was time for lights out.

She went into the yard and did her business
and we curled up on the bed
just before midnight.
She purred and purred for a long time.
I purred too in a human kind of way.
Then she went quiet and fell asleep.

Triangle

Triangle was a cute as can be
black and white kitten
home birthed from a cat called Blackie.
Blackie and I didn't get on.
She was a selfish lump of a cat,
disturbed and mind amiss.
I was glad when she left of her own accord.
Didn't know where she went and
frankly – didn't care.
But she did leave a few good kittens,
including Triangle, Black Tom
and Black and White.
Triangle was very warm
and very pick-up-able.
She had a white triangle on her face
with most of the rest of her being black.
You know when something
comes into your life
and you start loving it
and it loves you back
and even if it's just a cat
you like coming home to it.
Triangle and Black Tom were kittens
from Blackie's first litter
and they were growing and playing together.
They slept on my bed of course.
They would have been around four months
when I woke early one morning
and Black Tom was there by himself.

Triangle had gone.
She never came back.
No idea what happened.
Black Tom missed her as much as I did.
For days afterwards
he walked around the house
calling for her.

Two for White and Black

1 Nobody wanted him

if you lay your hands on him and let your fingers slide
along the invisible channels running through his fur
his warm ruffleable white and black envelope
if you feel the inflating and deflating of his body
knowing that his body does what yours does
filters air   pumps blood   maintains a temperature
if you try to draw out his ears and sense their flicking
            resistance
if you share the wish for life in his eyes
like me you'll wonder why nobody wanted him

how could it have been that nobody wanted him
when he would have *look-of-loved* back
into their devoting eyes
without dilution

his whole life

or theirs

2 Sounds I miss

the welcome home miaow
his feet padding quietly along the hallway
        then louder on the wooden floor
the minuscule squeak and rustle of the bed
        when he leaped upon it
the stretched-up scratching of his claws on the table leg
        as I opened his food
the crunch through cat biscuits
the quiet slap of his drinking
his high-pitched *this is my yard*
the celery crackle of mouse bones crunching
the scrape of his back and tail fur through the cat door
the metallic plink-plunk of his claws on the flyscreen
the soft thump when he'd jump to the desk
the twitchy drumming of his tail on the desk
the quiet ripple of his purr in our shoulder cuddle thing
our feline tête-à-tête
the broken carbie of his breathing that final day…

things

Coca Cola

red's passionate
white's pure
black's bad;
that's the can
and that's Coke –
and look how your hand
reaches out
and clicks around it;
the flowing script
is like a sperm tail
and that's for life;
yet being everywhere –
the most known thing on Earth –
it has something
of the plague in it;
pour it into a glass –
whole worlds, constellations,
spheres of light Big Bang
out of their cold black cell
foam in a creamy orgasm,
then, lighter and lighter
and bigger and bigger,
rush to their element –
the welcoming air

Stapler

basically
snake fangs in a long cold jaw
of chrome and coloured plastic;
a spring loaded barrel
on a hinge, light
and easy in the hand,
a perfectly completed design;
they're forever being whacked
softly on the head
but only rarely get thrown;
no one loves them enough
for really rough handling;
and over the years they too
have grown cool – especially
to paper, it's just a job;
they're usually old and restful
like slippers or a dog
that drifted in and stayed
to eat with you for years;
new ones get fondled of course
their dustless shininess
and bright red or blue admired;
electric ones evoke no feelings

Sellotape dispenser

don't knock me
for being grey solid and heavy;
there's nothing more useless
than a fluffy lightweight dispenser
tripping over itself
or dragging itself across the desk
when you pull the tape;
you need my resistance;
don't forget you're always
raving on about tension
being the cornerstone of life;
and I'm your man when it comes
to wrapping presents; I've never
told you but I can feel
the truth in your fingers;
it's there just before you cut
the tape across my jagging teeth;
your fingers tell me how much
or how little you love the person
you're giving the present to;
but I'll always keep it secret
so, come on, wrap the damned thing;
you can't fool your battered
old lump weight; only a fair job
this time – rough on the corners;
and you're so nervous with the card
the way you keep pressing down
that final bit of tape;
we quiet ones
often have the last word

Calculator

it looks like
a tiny mobile telephone
and it is usually right;
it only gets wrong numbers
if you do; there's an electronic
board inside with solder blob
terminals and join up wires;
each blob is like a football
stadium before the grand final;
hundreds of kids on the grass
holding up cardboard
with all the stadiums linked
by thirty metre television;
you want the square root
of eight hundred and thirty-five
and start pushing buttons;
the kids in the first stadium –
flutter flutter flutter;
the kids in the next stadium
see it on the big screen –
flutter flutter flutter;
and so it goes – all the way
down to the last stadium;
they'll get more kids
from interstate if they need them;
in less than half a second –
twenty-nine point one corrected;

it's right of course; it's always right;
and the new state of the art
models will march the kids back
to the dressing sheds
if they're not used
in the next five minutes

CD player

a lightweight black brick
with streamlined curves
and open mesh grids over
room surveying speakers;
spring loaded, sliding and re-
volving knobs and controls
in muted grey; one bright
red beam and a long yellow light;
the player doors glide open
like ports on a space station
and forty musicians
from France, Earth, lock in
and de-shuttle; revived from
deep space sleep they need no
warm up but straight away –
and very passionately – perform
the songs of water, wind and moon
from old, centuries dead Debussy

Filing cabinet

a tall cube, almost as high
as you are, bright orange but cold
when you first touch it; the only
round things are the lock cylinder
and the quiet plastic wheels
of the drawer tracks;
everywhere else it celebrates
flat surfaces, right angles and
the sliding in and out of things;
paper records, receipts and letters
in and out of manilla folders;
the manilla folders in and out
of their hanging sleeves;
the drawers in and out of the cabinet;
your past lies there so much more
neat and tidy than it really was;
every few years you'll get
the urge for spring cleaning
and after thinking about it a while
and putting it off a few times
you will get around to it;
suddenly you'll be throwing away
by the handful – Christmas cards,
vehicle bills, bank statements,
love cards – out, out, all out;
then you have the fresh open
rattly spaciousness of it;
the empty hangers slide back
and forth so easily; and you've
made a new set of labels
so you can do your future
so much better

Digital clocks

ignore the dull Romantics
waffling on about old clocks
and the hands of time and
claiming the little red lights
lack history or character;
fond and spooky stories
will be told about them too;
the night the alarm beeped off
three hours early and we woke
to a burning house but everyone
got out OK; or the day
it stayed at three twenty-seven
for an hour and kept pulsing
bright red all evening and later
that week we heard the news
from Canada; or the hot summer
night it just fell off the desk
and bending down to pick it up
you saw the shiny black spider
with its front legs raised;
the halogen lights of time
are here to stay; before
long they'll be in museums,
a specialist shop in Little Collins,
a website, a weekly Zoom

Children's clock

Donald Duck laughing and
bright yellow numbers – at last
you're having fun with me;
were you scared of me all those
centuries (your concept) when
you had to have the deathish
black numbers on my face;
and you left yourself wide open
when you made the starting point
at the top – such reverence;
further, don't you find it strange
that my hands are never
perfectly horizontal together;
does it show a lack
of real rest in your life;
and when you see me seem
to smile at one fifty and
frown at three forty – well,
they're your mood swings not mine;
come here…listen to me…
when you can tell me
what happens between
one second and the next
we'll talk again;
in the meantime,
here's to Donald Duck
and the big yellow numbers

The old moon

what if the moon
started doing its own thing;
stayed full for a week;
went back east after midnight
or later if it felt like it;
or in a single night
changed phase randomly
every hour like a slide show
to please its own dial;
could you care for an old
dead planet showing off like
some white-faced neon tripping
pizza in the sky;
care as much as you do
for the regular one;
the bright enough predictable
slowly changing old moon
that's always,
always, where it says it'll be

Rainbows

look at the rainbows
floating on the oil
in the gutters
when it's raining;
all the bright colours
reds and purples and greens
bending around
and circling and looping
as smooth and supple
as the bodies of cats;
oil from cars and trucks
and big throbbing
government buses;
but well before that
from the Earth's decay,
from change and compression;
rainbows, millions of them,
squashed in the Earth
for more years than we can grasp;
rainbows pumped from the ground
in dark grey sludge,
shipped to refineries,
boiled and piped and purified,
bottled and poured
into the black holes of motors;
and then the leaking out,
that sense of breathing again;
the relief and freedom
of dancing in the gutters
for children on rainy days

Black purse

she is not really listening
to the talk of the friends
she is sharing the square
white table with in the old
half restored pub;
she is staring at her purse;
she is holding it
and enjoying the feel
of its soft black skin;
she is looking at it intently,
turning it over and over
as if it were ancient and wise;
it is an old loyal friend;
they've been in many rooms;
travels, parties, work;
and if not in the same room
then just down the hall
and she has, afterwards,
told it everything;
maybe it knows still more;
the bad artist who's always
chasing her is buying;
she puts her hand
over her lemon squash, shakes
her head and smiles him away;
then she slides the black purse
right in front of the glass;
she swims her fingers over both
and in a Madam Starlight voice
quietens the whole table with
Tell me, Tell me, Tell me

Handbag

handbag keeps things
things it's meant to
and things left and forgotten;
keys to last year's flat,
brown coins, tickets,
phone numbers
on torn corners of paper,
wrapping of pads and condoms;
it's all scuffling around
and slowly wearing out
like dead shells in a rock pool;
on the outside,
handbag is soft to touch
swollen and puffy
in smooth hand-sticking-to
black, brown or blue leather;
the inside is lined with red silk;
a slit between the two
opens and closes like a clam
with its mouth defined
in fake brass, chrome or gold

Hairbrush

plastic and flexible
it curves in upon its spikes
like an echidna that's still learning;
unlike a beer can it springs
back when you crush it
and there are no ill effects
from overuse; it works equally
well in your left or right palm
and teaming up with any mirror
shows its love for you
by getting strict with the natural
fall of your hair and compensating
for your barber's lack of art;
it gives a lot and asks little back
except an occasional de-fluffing;
as time goes by however
the spikes start breaking off
until the whole thing's not
much use any more; most people leave
them somewhere near the spot
of the last unremembered brushing
and get another one of the same
colour; people going bald
have mixed feelings about them

Biker jacket

try me on
unless you're chicken;
was I a little heavier
than you expected when you first
slid your arms in and shucked
your shoulders and tried to look
really cool as if you didn't need
to check the mirror; feel tough;
I'm not asking if you are;
I'm telling you to be;
I'm giving you front – a brash
extravagant folding back
and pushing out of black leather
with a long piranha zipper
on each side; if you've got it
I'll help you flaunt it; but don't
waste my time; don't embarrass
me with diffidence; put out;
I'm the weapon of your self-belief;
I'm armour if you're scared;
wear me and they'll all
get out of our way

Supermarket trolley

more than
a chromed cage open at the top;
there is always one skewed wheel
to give you a hint of its free will;
it exists to help your food
gathering but it does so without
any generosity; those long horizontal
stacks you find them in are not
football teams, not warm social
contracts of bent intercourse;
the slight curve in that
spine of silver vertebrae
has nothing to do with flexibility –
it's merely the result of airspace;
you are able to sit a two-year-old
in the fold-down parcel flap but
never – never – put one there;
pinched skin or a cut in the calf
will come from that or worse
if it should tilt and topple;
and they do; they escape as well;
you've seen them in the streets
on Saturday night and the catcher
going around in the one-eyed
tractor and the trailer
with the chains on the back;
they're cold; they don't care;
from them the Daleks came

Radio

he made an excessively
sturdy pine shelf
for it above the toaster;
it is only a small, neat, light
plastic box, mostly red,
with a thin chrome slug
for an aerial and other
small silvery chrome bits;
inside it waits the untirable
voice of everyone's friend;
switched on, it brings
the world into his morning;
he lives alone and, yes,
he talks to it a bit;
he'll thank it for a time call
or a weather report;
he'll disagree out loud
with the personal belief
of a talkback caller;
once when it gave him
an overnight cricket score
he'd wanted to hear
he was silent with joy;
he turned it off, picked it up
and hugged it; then he reached
into a drawer for a clean Chux,
rubbed up the shine on the aerial
and wiped the dust
out of all the crevices
of its warm red cover

Frame

you've brought home a pale gold
one (or maybe fierce black)
and the shiny rounded edges
of the perfectly straight sides
reflect darker things in long
pinstripes – a bit like
the colours of the tiger you're
putting in it; the precise mitres
of each corner tease your eyes,
drag them around all four time
after time; you know you couldn't
cut so fine to save your life;
then you put the picture in;
the tiger's face is like a coloured
inkblot of symmetry and mystery;
there are frames within frames;
the thin creamy almond border
of the eyes leads to the amber-
green iris that frames the black
pupils that hold more of selfish
hunger than the squiby artist
dared to show; he paints
no blood stained teeth,
no razor claws

Lectern

upright, totally black
like a coffin on its end;
theatrical licence allows you
when making any speech or even
reading a poem from behind me
to indulge yourself in a fantasy
of magnificent oratory;
my angled top is like a launching
pad from which you'll land
your words in the very heart
of the crowd; but even as you
clutch my sides and tense your legs
and tilt your head uncleishly
to your audience you are aware
that you're also hiding behind me
just in case your body tells
a different story to your words;
but I've been watching you
for a while now – you're
getting better all the time;
people are listening;
you'll pull away from me soon;
you'll step to the side but still
keep a hand on me or rest your
notes on me but refer to them
less and less each time; there'll
come a night you'll go on alone;
afterwards you might wistfully
drag your fingers along my side
as you pass me in the corridor;
later on I'll just be furniture

Lawnmower

a shiny curvy green thing
like a frog with wheels
and a long handle at the back;
big red teeth spelling
V I C T A at the front;
pull the cord; again; third time
it shudders, erupts into noise,
the loud roar of made life;
(born life is much quieter);
first, around the perimeter,
then the back-breaker – in and out
under the overhanging shrubs and
the little sloping bit right down
the end where the fence is leaning
and the ground's squelchy;
it's half an hour before
you're ready to spiral in and
reduce the dark green shag pile
to a flat lime green carpet;
and how that lime green expands
as you work up a sweat;
how clean, how hoovered it looks;
suddenly you're bouncing through
the last lap, slick and tight
around the home turn before
charging down the final straight
in a green blur of mowing high;

you switch off the hot frog
and shake out the catcher
one more time; but even as you
wheel the shiny grass flattener
up the concrete to the shed
and look back at your labours
and sigh with pride
the slashed grass is healing;
its white roots suck hard in the soil
and push the growing on – a recovery
so slow you can't measure it,
so strong you can't stop it,
so quiet only the worms can hear it

Axe

I don't muck about; straight in;
ironbark to balsa by lunchtime
if you've got the sweat for it;
I'm much more than a big
sharp rock on a digging stick;
I'm the first put-together-tool,
the first bit of one-plus-one-ing;
nothing could happen until I did
and everything's happened since;
hammer, spade, arrow, Sputnik
and SpaceX – rocks on sticks;
so don't leave me out in the rain
after the firewood's chopped;
my edge will blunt, my handle
split and you'll be cold;
but keep me cleaned, polished
and honed and we'll turn
ironbark to balsa by lunchtime

Taps

don't just look – feel
the uncluttered elegance
of the modern tap;
run your fingers up that tall
penile one; wrap your palm
around a spherical one; touch
gloves with the tough fist
of the cube tap; or if 'now'
taps glaze you get a remake
of an old brassie with a four
spoked handle and screw-in
hexagonal top; whichever,
when the bathroom's done
and you stand in the doorway
and modestly admire
how square you made the tiling
and how perfect the paintwork
your lover might squeeze
your hand and point out
a minuscule sack of water
about to drop from the tap spout
and remark how far it's come;
through the new copper pipes
up the side of your old house;
the street mains; the filtration
plant; through dark concrete
tubes; the open channel;

farther back, a deep cold dam
and before that, some
high place in the hills
where a stream starts;
a quiet patch of earth
that's always green and damp

Automatic vacuum cleaner

…and began to ask where
she went wrong as she came
home each night and heard the
post-Stravinsky cacophony of it;
a gleaming golden sphere, bigger
than a beach ball, antennas
everywhere and a sucking
tube-thing defining its front;
she'd come to loathe the self-
renewing batteries she'd invented
and the anti-theft force shield
that she hadn't programmed
to exempt herself;
hated also the small cubes
of hard dust like dry wombat poo
it dropped from its arse; sometimes it
would stop for a little while and
she would get a bit of sleep but
it always self-started again and
she'd be in post-Stravinsky hurt
for hours; it trapped her
at the end of the hall one night;
ghost-floating, dink-donk-buzzing;
she stood still and stared at it;
there was no way out but the Roman;
calmly and proudly she leaped upon
the force shield and the last sound
she heard was the warm loud humming
of her old drag-along Hoover

Mouse

thief quiet, skater quick, more
cunning than a gutter rat;
it'll sniff out the cheese
you want though a thousand
windows bar the way; click;
click-click; the retrievable
cheese lies waiting at the end
of God knows how many
one-two one-twos; hop on;
enjoy the ride; don't worry
about trail markers; you'll need
no unwinding ribbons, no hacked
trees; it's never lost;
this prince of the twitching whiskers
knows nothing of dead ends;
with its tail up it eats lab rats
for breakfast; all wrong turns
get re-processed; it's like holding
under your palm a pile of gold
to buy you out of any mud;
click; click-click; and so
friendly that when you slide
its little fang across the screen
it lets you feel you almost
understand how it works
and that you're in charge; like –
it's da mouse – you're da man

Electric radiator

today a kind of red, hot,
narrow fluorescent tube;
but in the beginning a long
wire spiralled tightly around
a thin cylinder or fat hub
of baked white clay; back
in the fifties older people would
insist there be a dish of water
in the room of thick-armed
lounge chairs whenever
the circular Hecla was glowing;
we don't need that any more;
these days we take our heat straight;
many people guide extension
leads through tight holes
in wall linings to set one up
in an outside toilet for winter
reading; it's often an old one
with a rusty reflector covered
in Alfoil; we've given up
wondering how the high pressure
rush of icy water from a dam
a thousand kilometres away turns
to heat at our feet; the redness
at the heart of it will always
come up; we know that now;
cats love them; advertisers
photograph them in sand
with basking grey lizards

Thongs graveyard

under a rocky overhang
at a small impeccable beach
way up the coastal wild
I came across
an open thongs grave
and counted nineteen –
all sizes and colours
red black blue yellow green
different styles –
and hardly a pair in the lot;
someone had paid respects
by covering them with long ropes
of beer coloured seaweed;
the dampness of the sand
they slept in came only
from a seeping chain of droplets
in the rock wall behind them
for their grave was high
and safe from the waves
and even the spray of the waves.

even so…

what if
the one in ten year storm
should reach up,
snatch them out to sea,
heave and pitch them
in its rollercoaster froth and foam
all through a long black night
and toss them back to shore
in the calm of morning;
surely the end
of all those muscling swells
would find them asleep
on a sunny beach
in a dream of walking,
of flicking dry sand again

Fireworks

on a small island in a big calm bay
two people sat at the end of a jetty
waiting for the new year's eve fireworks
to start on the mainland;
light from the nearby hills
reflected across the water;
it had been raining that week
and they thought the fireworks
might be cancelled but they'd
still gone down just in case;
he rested his arm across
her shoulders and they breathed in
the saturated air that hangs around
a jetty at midnight; an old warm
phrase was forming slowly
at the back of their minds
but they were too wary
to say it yet; neither wore
a watch so all they could do was wait,
hoping the fireworks would still happen
as they looked across the black water
and the light rippling over it;
at last they heard the car horns,
then Auld Lang Syne
from the restaurant on the point
and suddenly the whole scene
burst with colour; long spears
of pink, huge bombs of red and gold,

big spider webs of orange
and silver expanded and spent
themselves against the grey-black
cloudy sky; she clapped her hands
like a child and turned to him
and they smiled and hugged each
other and looked at each other
in the special way that people do
in the early days of love;
early days when the dried crust
of old loving flakes off bit by bit
and whatever's left of the heart
begins to remember what it was like
to be open and wanting and caring
and practises day after day
until it is again

Chrysler Regal Station Wagon

well here it is
my iridescent
crème de menthe
immaculate interior
genuine one owner
late 70s
low slung
hill eating
highway beast;
that soft
sultry
suspension
hugs the long
unwinding road
like paint;
nothing can stop it;
I reckon
I could drive it
underwater;
come on,
hop in,
buckle up;

the world's
our windscreen;

let's go

let's go

www.ingramcontent.com/pod-product-compliance
Lightning Source LLC
Chambersburg PA
CBHW070920080526
44589CB00013B/1386